With V.

CW00521439

Poetry Matters

A creation of one hundred plus poems
from Africa and the UK

From:

BY BEST SELLING AUTHOR

OLUSOLA SOPHIA ANYANWU

Sophia Anyanwu

Dedicated to the memory of my beloved sister,
Elizabeth Inyangete Adebayo

(January 1956 – May 2022)

"The grass withers, the flower fades,
but the Word of our God stands forever."
Isaiah 40:8, NASB

CONTENTS

DIRGES, ELEGIES AND NOTES

I SAW YOU

I saw you, a strong, sturdy stem,
Raising your branches and leaves
High in praise
Sure of more tomorrows

The cankerworm came,
Weakening the stem's strength
Your leaves aged prematurely—
Gradually plucked off in turns
Branches dried to twigs
Roots made redundant
Abandoned their duties

The sunlight brings no warmth,
The rain brings no refreshing
The wind brings no music
This is not winter's sleep
Tomorrow does not worry you
You return to Earth—
Your maker's Eden

TO MUMMY LIZZY

My darling Elizabeth Inyang Adebayo went home to Heaven on Saturday night, May 23rd, 2022. We were shocked and devastated by the gaping hole her life and memory will leave in our family, fellowship, and friends. However, we are eternally grateful that her end was peaceful – free of pain by God's mercy and a miracle – considering she was a cancer patient. We are also eternally grateful that she is now in the presence of our Saviour, our Lord Jesus Christ, whom she deeply loved, truly served, and loyally worshipped.

Mummy Lizzy (as I fondly called her) lived a full 66 years and four extra months. She overflowed with intelligence, hospitality, and motherhood, and was a friend to the fellowship of believers of the most high God. 'Yeshua' was always the emblem on her phone and social media. She began work as a brilliant scientist in 1982 and then became a gifted lawyer in 2000. She retired in 2011 when first diagnosed with cancer, which was successfully treated. She then devotedly served as a social carer till February 2022. Until her end, she was a creative writer of prayers, a great cook, a loving mother, a devoted wife, a loving grandmother, and so much more – as you will read and agree with me in the poems, excerpts and tributes to her blessed memory.

Despite the depth of her personality and her cheerful demeanour, she could be an introvert, preferring to keep things to herself and sharing with the Lord only. However, she had a very great sense of humour and kept a smile perpetually on her face. If she was not smiling, she was in deep rapport with her Yeshua.

Her working life was impressive. Apart from giving counsel and advice to people on a government level, she ministered to a number of people spiritually and had great impact on them. For example, her being a good and humble wife to my brother served as an example to the younger wives in the Brethren fellowship. The virtues of marriage and the proverbial wife of Proverbs 36 was her model. The number of people I saw lovingly showering devotions of prayers and gifts upon her and the family in the last weeks of life is a testimony.

I loved her way of creating unique nicknames for members of the family and the fellowship. Growing up in Western Nigeria enabled her to pick the Yoruba language, which was an asset in her marriage. She gave her children the Yoruba names they bear: 'Oluwafeyikemi' for Christabel, and 'Dotun' for Alex. She did not ever impose her own Calabar culture on the family and strictly followed her husband's wishes in the way their children were disciplined – the Word of God FIRST.

I will mostly miss her gentle, humble spirit, her humility in the Lord, her faithful devotion to the Brethren and family of God, her encouraging words for every and any situation, her care of her husband and children for 38 years – putting God first. The fact that she sacrificed her birthday every year for the last 24 years, and spent them with the Lord instead, leads me to believe that it was her behind the idea of having her wedding reception at the local orphanage. *'She put God first in everything,'* I heard her husband, my brother, saying as she lay on her death bed. *'Thank you, Liz, for pointing the family to Lord Jesus in your joyful devotion towards God.'*

We are eternally grateful to God for the legacy of peace she gave us in her last weeks of life, astounding the staff at both the hospital and hospice. There was no twisted agony and pain. She let us dwell in the joyful presence of Christ as we prayed, sang songs, worshipped in fellowship, gathering in unity with family, friends and loved ones from all over the world. Brethren whose lives she had impacted came from the US, Nigeria, and other places outside the UK to bless her on her death bed.

Because of the legacy of faith she left behind, we can all look forward to the day we will all see her again in Heaven with our Papa God. And in her absence, we celebrate life knowing that "Because of the Lord's great love, we are not consumed, for His compassions never fail. They are new every morning. Great is His faithfulness." (Lamentations 3:22 -23)

May we continue to relive her memory in eternal joy and gratitude.

Amen.

CANCER THOUGHTS?

At night, when all sleep,
Even your spouse is asleep—
You wake, knowing he's asleep.

What are your thoughts
Of the cancer you know,
Hiding in the shadow of death?

Waiting like a sly predator
Waiting to greedily take over
Your body.

Waiting like a landlord
To evict you out of
Your earthly body

What are your thoughts
On the cancer you know,
Sending threats of an untimely end?
Does your mind go to that end?

My hon without me
My hon a widower
My son without his mother
My daughter without her mother
My grands without me

My dear God, why me?

UNLESS A SEED FALLS

Unless a seed falls
There will be no rebirth
Unless a seed falls
There will be no resurrection
Unless a seed falls
The earth will be barren
Unless a seed falls
Multiplication will not happen

Unless a seed falls
Nature is abused
Unless a seed falls
The new won't burst forth
Unless a seed falls
The tree will not emerge
Unless a seed falls
Its fruit won't be seen

Unless a seed falls
Its kind won't be produced
Unless a seed falls

God's glory won't be seen
Unless a seed falls
Its testimony won't be given
Unless a seed falls
The Son's purpose is futile

Unless a seed falls
Man's population diminishes
Unless a seed falls
The sower will not sow
Unless a seed falls
There'll be no harvest
Unless a seed falls
Continuity will see its end

Unless a seed falls
There'll be no eater
Unless a seed falls
God's work on Earth is done
Because a seed fell
There is creation
Because a seed fell
There is salvation

MUMMY LIZZY

Your strength decreased,
Not your peace—

You are pressed
But not crushed
You are battered
But not defeated

Your health's taken,
But not your faith

Your kidney stopped,
But not your fervour for Him
Your speech ceased,
But not your perseverance
Your liver stopped,
But not your hope

You were broken—
But not your heart.

You walked in death's valley,
But you were victorious
You saw death's shadow
But weren't dismayed

You had cancer Terminal 4
But it didn't touch your spirit
In your pain, there were no tears
In your ashes, there was beauty

A PRAYER FOR YOU

You are restored,
There is hope in your future
You are well,
You are strong in your strength
Goodness and mercy are following you
You will be surprised by God's goodness
He will free you from every affliction,
AMEN.

Lord God Jehovah
We are so blessed to have you as our Father—
You are teaching us to trust in you.

Whatever seasons we go through,
In sickness or in health
You are trustworthy, faithful and merciful
You are compassionate, kind, caring
You are loving and full of grace

Take our burdens of fear, weakness and doubt—
You are our burden carrier.

Cause us to continue to trust You,
Cause us to remember Your Word
That all things will work for our good
That Your grace is sufficient for us
That nothing is impossible for You
That Your promises are Yes and Amen.

Help us stay strong in faith
And in Your Peace, knowing that
You are able, in Lord Jesus Christ's name,
Amen.

ELIZABETH ADEBAYO, WOMAN OF GOD

E – Energetic, Eager, Enlightening
L – Loyalty, Loving, Lively
I – Inspirational, Intercessor, Intelligent
Z – Zealous, Zest, Zeal
A – Amazing, Anointed, Appreciative
B – Beautiful, Blessed, Blessing
E – Evangelist, Endurance, Excellence
T – Truthful, Triumphant, Treasured
H – Humble, Helper, Honest

FINAL EXIT

YES, God is omnipresent
All powerful and omniscient
He is invisible,
No one sees Him.
We did not see
When He took away
Mummy Lizzy

Everyone gathered at the hospice
Waiting to hear her final breath of bye
Everyone daily by her bedside
Waiting for that final exit,
Or a miracle
Praying along, giving final comfort

Death is cold,
Death squeezes the last breath
Gripping greedily with hands
That know no mercy—
Hands that know only duty
TAKE THE BREATH OF LIFE AWAY!

Suddenly you gasp...
All your life you have breathed
Consciously and unconsciously
Awake and asleep

Finally, it is all taken and
You are transported to another life
in glory

IN GLORY

Breath is not needed here
You are no longer flesh and bone
You are full spirit
You live like Papa God

Heaven, like electric cars,
Needs no fuel
Heaven, like the sun,
Gives solar energy
Heaven has no darkness
There is sun and moon
in Heaven

Time is continuous
You don't need sleep or get tired
There is so much to see and do

Each new day is different
Each new day is a higher glory
Each new day an explosion of joy

Eternity is sweeter than anything
You have all your heart's desires
All fulfilled in glory

Eternity is the best thing
This is what you have
Mummy Lizzy!

Praise the Lord!

QUEEN ELIZABETH II

Hail Queen,
A woman like me—
Not a Nigerian like me
Not a commoner
A lover of God like me
A dog lover like me
Not a black woman
Not a migrant
A mother of a nation
A platinum monarch

Not a divorcee
Not a single mother
You created history
You ended an era
Not in Africa or Europe—
In Britain

You have left
Your footprints
In the epochs of time.

On 8 September 2022
You reignite my memory
Of my loss of
Elizabeth Adebayo
On 22 May 2022
A lawyer, a carer
A mother, grandmother
My beloved sister
A queen like you
In Crayford Castle
A monarch like you
In her palace
At 17 Valley Road

You both will meet
In Heaven
Without your
Earthly crowns
And earthly glory
As you both enter
Into the rest
He has called you.

Enjoy divine rest
Enjoy divine knowledge
Enjoy celestial glory

Enjoy your new rebirth
Enjoy heavenly splendour
Enjoy the holy presence
With your Creator

STORMS OF LIFE

Dear Papa God,
Help me to trust You always
Teach me to trust Your Word always

When the storms of life rage against me
Help me to remember You are with me
In that boat tossing wildly unto death
Help me to experience peace
Because you are there and near

Hear my heart's cry
Please still every doubt and fear
Whispered from the enemy's lips
Into my vulnerable mind – that
You are not there with me
Teach my mind to always remember
That You are with me and for me

Even when death slays me
I know You remain
The Light in that darkness

PERPLEXED

Where am I, Lord?
This cannot be Heaven, Lord
I am still in my old body, Lord
This cannot be earth, Lord
I can't see family and friends
Is this paradise, Lord?
I'm just aware of my mind

What do you call this place, Lord?
I speak, but not audibly, Lord
Am I trapped in my body, Lord?
I lie still on the bed, Lord
Am I in a coma, Lord?
I hear voices from my beloved—
How he so wishes I return to him
He sorrows inwardly all day and night,
Prayers remain constant under his every breath

I hear my daughter pleading for a miracle, Lord,
She's distraught, devastated and disoriented
My son is too heartbroken, Lord,

His sorrow and grief break his heart, Lord
I hear the cries of the saints day and night,
Urging and pleading with You, Lord

I am at peace here, Lord!
I can't see you yet, Lord!
I know your plans for me, Lord
They are good, Lord
Tell my heart not to be afraid, Lord
You are taking my life, Lord
You are setting me apart from reality, Lord

You are separating me from all
That I have ever known and loved.
You're closing the door you opened to me
Sixty-five years ago, Lord.
You are taking me away
From my home, family and fellowship, Lord
You are taking me to a new home,
As You did for Abraham

You crushed your own son, Lord.
He pleaded with You,
But Your decision prevailed, Lord
Still my heart in confidence, Lord

Soak me in Your boldness, Lord
Fill me to overflowing with my faith in You, Lord

Are You slaying me, Lord?
I feel the intense pain of leaving
My earthly glory
I feel the unbearable pain of
My loved ones
I feel excruciating pain from losing
My family and loved ones

My journey to You is near, Lord
You are holding my hands, Lord
Goodbye, my beloved.
Goodbye, my children.
Goodbye, my family.
Goodbye, my grandchildren.
Goodbye, my Brethren Fellowship family.
I am in safe hands and
Will see you all tomorrow.

Papa God,
I am ready,
Lord!

GOOD NIGHT

Be at rest, oh my soul
The Lord has crowned me
With His favour, goodness,
Hope and faithfulness

He gives me peace,
And His comfort
He didn't give me a spirit of fear but
Of love and a
Sound mind to glorify
His name from
Morning till night

Whatever is happening
Or has happened, Your will
Has been done
Thank You for being with
Me right now
I don't understand my illness—
I truly don't understand why
This disease hasn't bowed

To Your name
Still my soul will bless You
I believe that even now
You can restore me
But if this is what will be
I say goodnight in the hope
Of hearing You say
"Well done, my faithful daughter,
Come into my rest."

Goodnight, Papa God
I will lie down in peace
May I wake in the morning
To Your realm of glory
Forever more in eternity.

ON THAT DAY

On that day
When You say come,
I will come because
I have no choice
I have no say
I have no options
I am powerless
I am helpless
I can't decide
I can't ask why

I can't refuse
I will come because
I am mortal
You are immortal
I will come because
It's not my will
It's Your will

I will come because
You hold the key

To all mysteries
I will come because
You are my creator
I will come because
You decide my fate

I will come because
It is Your decision
I will come because
I am the clay
You are the potter
I will come because
You are God

STILL WITH US

Shiny skin glowing with
The softness and sheen of a newborn
She is asleep, not dead
Curly black hair
Soft, shiny, silver-streaked
Cuddles her head
Frames her face
Her eyes are shut to life
In a sleep so deep
As a baby

Wakeful to brief moments
Of whispers of love
Of whispers of endearment
Of whispers of encouragement
Offered as food for her soul
Her eyes twitch open
Her lips part to smile
Very, very subtle
In approval...

19/09/2022 –
QUEEN ELIZABETH II LAID TO REST

You were a monarch
Who made history in death
You nearly clocked a century
The crown sat seventy years on your head
Then the tenor bell rang
On 8th September 2022

Your breath ceased on this day
As you tasted death
You were taken down in style
On a century-old carriage
Attended to by six thousand officers
From the three armed forces
Three thousand military personnel
Black-uniformed officers
Watch guards
Palace guards
Grenade guards
Pall bearers

Ninety-eight naval officers
Ten thousand police officers

A procession of black horses and
Black limousines
Three funeral services to send you off;
First at Westminster Abbey
Second at Windsor Castle and
Third and privately at St George's Chapel

It was a glorious procession to each one,
The Royal Navy in white caps and blue jackets
Carrying your bier from Buckingham Palace
To Westminster Abbey
British flags lined the streets

You passed by the Tower of London
You passed St James's Cathedral
And the crowd of people
The elderly, the young, children and babies
Graced the roads in throngs of thousands
Day and night
Having queued hours and hours to glimpse you
Lying in state
They lined the roads and fields,
Waving at you

Kissing you with bouquets of flowers
On your bier
On your path
Offering prayers
A hundred presidents and heads of governments
graced your funeral.

At Windsor Castle,
The Sebastopol Bell tolled ninety-six times
Faithfully marking your life on Earth
Your corgis Mick and Sandy mourned you
Emma wailed and barked her farewell
It was a cloudy day at fifteen degrees
The trees looked greener
Your royal wreath a marriage of
Myrtle, rosemary
Gold, burgundy, white, pink and purple

At St George's Chapel
You were laid to rest eternally
The Archbishop of Canterbury
Gave you his blessings
The Dean of Windsor
Blessed your soul with a prayer
From Revelation 21
For its final journey to Heaven

As a Christian soul
You were properly prepared
To meet the King of kings
The emblem and mark of
Your sovereignty and power
Your purple velvety crown
Studded with pearls of silver and gold
And red, green and blue diamonds
Was taken off you

You were divested of your orb
To signify the end of your earthly rule
Your staff of office was broken
To symbolise the end of your reign
The motet was played for you
After the lowering of your casket
As your piper played an epithet
My eyes dropped tears
Of farewell

DON'T CRY FOR ME

I am out of the box
I am not six feet down
You can't see me
You won't recognise me
Like they couldn't recognise
The Lord's reappearing
Youth dresses me again
Never will I ever feel
Grief, pain, fear and sickness
Don't cry for me

You will see me again
Where memories of my earthly life
Are but shadows of vapour
I see what you will behold some day—
The heart of the Lord
The revealer of all mysteries and truths
Don't cry for me

My soul and all my being
Live now in blessed eternal glory

Have a glimpse of revelation
When you get sick and health is dripping
When your faith doesn't bring healing
When your prayers don't change a thing
When your good works seem for nothing
Like "He bore all your pain and sickness" isn't
existing
You see all the negatives still lingering
Your tiredness, weakness and helplessness
Aren't leaving
When in your emotions you are drowning
Don't cry for me

I'm seated with the Most High
In the sacred secret place of our Lord
In security, love and protection
Here, there are no trials and troubles
There are no wars, retrenchment or lack
There are no more drips and pills to take
I am completely healthy, young and strong
Don't cry for me

I can never shed tears
I will never know unhappiness
I walk on streets of gold
I am surrounded with fathomless perfection

I hear the most glorious melodies
I glow in awesome and dazzling beauty
I have everything I ever wanted
I am united with family, saints, angels and Christ
I see your future with me again
Because He conquered death
Don't cry for me

REALITY DAWNS

There's a vacant seat
At our dining table
You won't ever sit
There's an empty space
On my bedside
You will never embrace
There's an absence
On my birthday
You can't give your presence
There's just me
On our wedding anniversary
You never can share with me

There's Christmas this year
Without you near me
You can't give new memories here
The summer is lustreless
In our garden
You won't ever harness
There's a cheerless autumn fall
In our home

Your laughter will never fall
There's a wintry winter
At Valley Road
You'll never walk the road
There's no mirth this spring
In our living room

You'll never cook up surprises
There's a gap
At our fellowship
You'll never partner with me
There are pangs of pain
In my heart
You'll never be with me on Earth
There's a new reckoning
In my soul
Our reunion in Heaven
Someday

DEATH BED THOUGHTS

They say I'm dying
The thought frightens me not
But why not?

Where are all those worries
From family, fellowship and work?

I remember them not
Or those thoughts
Of tomorrow's plans for holidays
I think them not
Or those agendas
To make phone calls and visits
I care not
Or to do the day's priority list
Of returning text messages
Of gratitude, forgiveness and evangelism
I remember them not
Or time to pray for brethren and family
I think not

But now I understand with revelation
In my weakness, You are strong
You carry all my burdens
Of thoughts, worries and plans
So I don't have to, instead
I feel the weight of peace
You have filtered
Pain, panic, fear, sorrow and grief
From my heart
You have swelled my heart with
Divine thoughts of
Your reward to me, your saint

By day, You have shielded me daily
With the love of the saints
Encompassed around me
By night, You feed me with the music
Of prayers from the saints
Blessing my heart with bliss
My soul is in hope, assuring me
That I will not drown
Or be burned
But will see the salvation
You have planned for me

THE VISIT

I visited you today
I stepped in
To your hospital ward
I saw you but
It didn't seem to be you
Dressed in skin layers
Of a century
Your eyes stared at me
But said nothing

You saw me
Trying to be brave
I prayed for you
I embraced you
You remained silent
I asked for your smile
Your right lower lip
Moved very slightly
Towards the right
For a second
You saw me for the last time

My sister stepped in
To visit you today
She didn't recognise you
Your appearance shocked her
It brought sorrow to her
You saw her rush out in haste
Gushing tears from her eyes
After her brief farewell hug
You saw her
for the last time…

ECO POETRY –
NATURE, WAR,
ENVIRONMENT, CLIMATE

GHOSTS FROM UKRAINE

Smoke billows in the sky
Couples quarrel about leaving or staying
It is cold, freezing
No light, no water
People hide in basements like rats in fear
Expecting to be caught or waiting for a miracle of
rescue

Ukraine – they have lived here all their lives
It is the loss of a built kingdom
It is the loss of many souls
Emblems of memories:
The streets, neighbours, pictures, schools, churches
All wiped away by one evil Russian blow

Genocide against innocent people
Atrocities committed because they stand by their
rights
Outrageous actions of war to humanity
To bring them to their knees
To strip them of their dignity

To soak them in sacrificial blood

The world holds Ukraine in prayer
Alms of comfort, provision and support
As war crimes escalate
Thousands of evacuees are uprooted
Disrupted permanently of their world
Now in explicable fear of tomorrow

Friends, family, fellowship
All separated by missiles
Like the coronavirus, the Russians move
From Kyiv to Bucha, to Khorkiv
Spreading their plague and poison
As victims are bathed in their blood

From bombs that shatter love, peace, joy, tranquillity
and life
Lives, memories, loved ones are meshed in war
Reducing victims of war to underground burrowed
creatures
Russians assault victims as Ukrainian musicians play
the violin
Ukrainians sing for victory and hope
Ukrainians unite as one to fight the Russian plague

The Russian plague rages as cities are emptied of
people
City landmarks are demolished
Cities are roasted in fire
Survivors escape to nearby cities
Their generation must hand over
The baton of hope and victory to the next generation

Mass graves in Bucha
Men taken from their homes
Mutilated, butchered and unfit for burial
Widows, widowers, orphans are created
Fatherless, motherless, childless are created
And the aged?
They will become the Ghosts of Ukraine

CHANGE

Embrace me though you find my arms cold
Though to you my open arms seem old
They are wisdom ingrained for you to take hold
Embrace a friend, not a foe, so be bold
I won't banish your silver but offer you gold
I don't come to change your ways of old
Be patient as you see what will enfold
From your having both ways, you can mould

NIGERIA IS NOT FORGOTTEN

Oh my Nigeria
I pray for you
I dream of you.

I haven't forgotten the land of my youth,
fertility and wealth
I left you during the twentieth century
Salaries were three months overdue
Education was not free, still not free

I haven't forgotten the land
of my forefathers,
culture and tradition
I once saw you in glory—
Before that cloud of Biafra War broke you
Leaving the ugly spirits of poverty,
greed and disunity

I haven't forgotten the land of my upbringing,
family and memories
I once enjoyed electricity and water

Before corruption turned these to
darkness and dryness
Artificial blackout and drought

I haven't forgotten the land of my dreams,
desires and devotions
I once enjoyed good roads
Before corruption turned them to death gullies
Untarred bumpy roads and hours of holdup

I haven't forgotten the land of my garden,
farms and neighbours
I left when you had become destitute
Daily living and feeding a struggle
You couldn't feed, clothe or care for your own

I haven't forgotten the land of my dogs,
cats and chickens
In the dark years of lack
You broke me on every side
It was hard watching family famishing
I learnt to beg, borrow and be brave

I haven't forgotten the land of my hope,
my desires and prayers
You bred thugs, occultists, rogues and murderers

In your chaotic system
I couldn't bear the hatred, disunity and
discouragement
I had to flee to a haven of safety

I haven't forgotten the land of my faith
Created by God
I still think of you in my thoughts
I still remember you in my memory
I still love you in my heart—
I still pray for you

I HAVE A DREAM FOR NIGERIA

People will not depend on
secondhand clothes
Salaries and pensions will be
promptly paid
The light bulbs will come on
from the switch
Water will gush out at the tap's turn
The tarmac roads will be smooth
and solid
Begging will cease

Homes for the homeless
Care homes for the aged
Nigerians will be united in peace
Nigerians will enjoy freedom
In the North, South, East and West
Investors will invest in Nigeria
Petroleum will feed Nigeria
Gold and coal will sustain Nigeria
Agriculture will boost Nigeria

Postal systems will deliver
Train and plane services will work
Joblessness and strikes will die
Criminality and evil acts will stop
Free education will reign
Nigerians will laugh again

Free health service for Nigerians
No more tears on faces of Nigerians
Nigerians will build Nigeria
My dream for Nigeria is—
Nigeria will flourish – Yes!
My prayer for Nigeria is
Nigeria will be one—
AMEN.

THAMESMEAD (an acrostic poem)

Town houses join their hands in unity,
holding together different nations
in the south, east, north and west of Thamesmead—
shopping at Lidl and Sainsbury's in the south,
the town centre in the north
Omo and Ade's in the west
Costcutter in the east

Having been created
from the blessed hands of River Thames
Flowing still through the land
its reclaimed land is a new haven
a mead pregnant with more promises
more future aspirations and achievements
of talented people from all walks of life

And they bring music, art, culture, language,
food, dance, education, faith,
varied talents in every area of humanity
forming a talented people
uniting unique personalities

merging a multicultural society
creating a blessed community

Meeting needs, expectations of its residents
Through collaborative services of its landlords
Gallions and Peabody
equipping locals and residents with trades, careers,
quality housing, safe green areas
volunteering opportunities for all
making funding available for talents

Everyone's opinion is sought
for new ideas of expansion, creativity and well-being
in Thamesmead north, south, east and west
for inhabitants who span Bexley and Greenwich
boroughs
engaging arts, crafts, music, poetry, writing and dance
organised by TACO and associates to bring the
communities
to live better and together in health, safety and unity

Safety is guaranteed
through friendly, competent neighbourhood staff
from the police, ministers of the gospel
Southmere, Birchmere, swans and all parks are safe
developing and regenerating to eliminate

crime, undeveloped space, joblessness
and youth demoralisation for a
safe and healthy London and South East

Merging of the two housing trusts
Peabody and Gallions
have birthed a new library, health centre,
a lakeside boating experience, carnivals, shopping
centres,
a culture directory of Arts
affordable two-, three-, and four-bedroom houses
giving affordable rent as tenants live
a surreal experience

Ever growing with new ideas
for developing better new houses, new parks,
new gardening, new leisure play areas,
new quality of life for Thamesmead inhabitants
engulfing residents in a new world
far from the original Thamesmead world
of years ago

Abbey Wood Station and the Thamesmead
you knew in the twentieth century is a far cry from
what it is in the twenty-first century
what with being a foodbank centre and

everyone is rushing to be tenants,
jumping onto buses
180, B11, 401, 244, 177 and 229
to belong to this golden community
once conceived as a crime zone and no-go area

Do you know what?
The best will yet come for Thamesmead residents
a Queen Elizabeth Line in its midst, taking residents
to work
in style and comfort to Canary Wharf,
Paddington, and Heathrow,
in the briefest of time, though diverse in their ideas
in unity, the town houses they live in
string them along together in peace, respect,
inclusion and love.

A TRIBUTE TO MY MOTHERLAND

On the one hand
I have so many reasons to bless Nigeria
I look back over the forty-four years
spent in different parts of the country,
as I recall moments
of joy, bliss and fulfilment

It was the only home
I had in the whole world—
where I did not think
I was different from anyone else
where I experienced freedom
without knowing its value
where I knew that I was not alone
in my lack or abundance of God's blessings

When there was electricity supply
everyone else like me enjoyed the light
When there was a salary delay
I was not alone in this affliction

Even when there was scarcity of fuel
I was not alone

Whatever afflicted me afflicted everyone
When there was no hold up on the roads
and the light was extended for a few more hours
or even the ending of some national strike
my fellow Nigerians and I enjoyed the privilege

There was always a group I could belong to,
identify with, fit in and be comfortable
Nigeria is home, regardless of my religion,
career, ethnicity or status
I never felt uncomfortable
Pidgin English levelled everyone down socially.

On the other hand
I have withheld my blessings
when in disillusion and pain
I sorrow with over four million Nigerians
across the Planet Earth
for being let down and having to
leave Nigeria.
Permanently? I hope not!

INTERDEPENDENCE

We marvel at the ants
They have built themselves a palace
Architectural structure leaves us dumbfounded
They are so tiny
Their mansion so huge, vast and mighty
We wonder

The animals marvel at man
They have built themselves empires
Their creativity and intelligence
dumbfounds them
Man is in dominance of everything
They are not the strongest
The iron, steel, technology, skyscrapers
They wonder

We marvel at creatures like the hyena
They have a marvellous community spirit
Their hierarchy and leadership qualities
leave us dumbfounded
They are not the most powerful or intelligent

Their unity and achievement are incredible
We wonder

The animals are shocked at man
The empires they build, they destroy
The kingdoms and their dwelling areas, they destroy
They are survivors of war but repeat history in peril
They create and use indiscriminate weapons and
decimate their numbers
Changing and endangering the peaceful circle of
nature and life
They wonder…

THE MENU TODAY

The sky is blue, almost
but for a scattering and sprinkle
of white clouds
The droning of airplanes
The squawking of crows and magpies

Traffic is heavy and
about to erupt
like a volcano spreading
lavas of cars all over
Harrow Manor Road
Lidl down the left corner
Sainsbury's in front of me
Builders are building new homes

I cross over, reaching the junction—
Londis shop and petrol station
Abbey Wood Station all on my route
My focus changes
I walk fast on Felixstowe Road
The road to my daily labour

GOD WITH ME IN THE FIRE (incident in Nigeria, March 2022)

My enemies ambushed me
Surrounded me like hungry wolves
Waiting to devour my flesh
Like a flood to carry me
On its waves to my grave
They captured me
A helpless woman as a new-born babe
Freshly widowed on the day
My love's corpse freshly cool
I became like a prey
Whose attackers hurled
Heavy stones of allegations, painful as darts
Of killing my love
Who in our love nest
His breath ceased in the throes of lovemaking

I was stripped to the skin
Their eyes feasted on my womanhood
My pride turned to shame
My sanctuary invaded, desecrated

They paraded me in scorn
Round the village, barefoot
As witch, murderer…
My mind flashes back in reels—
How was I not stoned to death?
How was my body left unbruised?
How was my face left unscarred?

My nakedness to the world was
The revenge they sought
My family name slurred in mud
My children's hearts broken, crushed
Their future happiness splintered
In pieces like broken China glass
Will they ever recover from
The shame, shock, humiliation
The brutalising agony and nightmares witnessing
Their mother's public execution of her pride and
sanity

Papa God was in the fire with me—
I did not cry tears
I did not utter a word
I did not plead mercy
I did not shield my nakedness
I called to my God for justice

He is my truth
He stood in the fire with me
He sent an angel to vindicate me
To free me from the prison of false accusations

I was in fire
The fire didn't burn me
My flesh didn't smell of smoke
God carried my cross
He didn't let its weight crush me
I wandered like the Israelites
Round and round the town
For twenty-four hours
My flesh didn't give up on me
It banished all comforts, desires, longings
All urges the flesh craved for
It didn't cry from aches, weariness or the soul's pain
I didn't choke or drown in my sorrow
Their flames of hatred didn't consume me
The lament, wails of my children pierced my ears
They were totally powerless against
a throng a thousand plus strong
steeped in their blind and binding ignorance
turning them to savages in their jungle justice
like the faithful few Jews on Good Friday

my children and family were crippled with fear and
helplessness
in the tide of vicious hatred, blatant evil from
the god of evil

You were in the fire with me
in the pit of ignorance
my accusers had dug themselves in
You raised the light that brought unexpected
sunshine
and ended the sorrows of the night
The light came with joy in the morning
that chased the evil darkness
of repression, ignorance, illiteracy
Unveiling the true death of my love
Educating the world with knowledge
That I was no witch, no murderer
My love had died of cardiac arrest
From taking Viagra to make our intimacy sweet

HUNTER AND MOUSE

Hunter, you have been blessed
You have an elephant on your head
You carry an antelope on your shoulder
You strap a buffalo on your back
Yet with your toes
You want to trap a mouse!

The mouse dodged your toes
Now you resort to war
On the entire mouse family
Will this acquire more lands
Produce mineral resources
Increase your wealth
Enrich your population
Create nuclear weapons?

This action will be your doom
Will leave a stain on your history
Will expose you to the world's wrath
Your generation will curse the day
You waged war on the mouse

Its fame will increase
Like an underground seed
Ready to burst out in foliage and bloom
But your fame will decrease
Becoming appalling
Like the stunted growth of
A malnourished child

As the death toll rises from hunger
And poverty strikes the young, old
And innocent victims from your poison
You will leave a cursed legacy
Of stench from the innocent blood
Crying out for justice and revenge

VICTIMS OF PERSECUTION

The suffering church in Nigeria
The north of Nigeria
Facing persecution for Jesus
And rejection for Jesus
The young maidens of Chibok
The young maidens from the north
Abducted in one night
Away from family and friends
Away from the church of Christ
Away from their families

They cried for help
But rescue did not come
They cried to God
He saw and heard them
He gave them grace to survive
And the will to testify
And the courage to keep faith

The government of Nigeria
Failed them

The army did not rescue them
Their schools failed them

One victim is Agnes,
Now nineteen years old
Now a mother of two
Forced to Islam against her own faith
God rescued her back to her world
But her own did not receive her
Faced with rejection from family
Faced with the fruits of rape
Faced with abandonment from Nigeria
Faced with disruption of education

I ask, Agnes, how are you?
You are still young
You have hope
You have faith
You have God
You will testify very soon

Chibok victims, how do you fare?
Our prayers continue to hold you
The suffering church in Nigeria
How do you persevere?
How do you feel for Nigeria?

The suffering church in Nigeria
Needs your prayers, your love
Your support and your faith
Agnes and the rest will testify
To the goodness of God

PONDER

Have you ever sat still under the sun
for seconds and let the sun's rays
shower its warmth over you
while you soak it all in
on a cold spring day in February?

Most trees are still naked.
Few beginning to bud, ready to
spring back eagerly to glory.
Do you wonder about the sun's rays
Incubating life within?

Have you ever marvelled
How the cold and warmth work in unity?
The sun shines, spreading its heat
bathing one in a hot bath
The breeze blows its enticing kiss
It's a cold spring day in February.

COVID HISTORY

'I can't hear!' you say.
'You are mute,' you say.
'I hear you now,' you say.

'I can't hear songs,' God says.
'My face mask seals my mouth,' I say.
'No singing allowed in church,' I say.

'The mask is now off,' you say.
'I prefer working from home!' I say.
'We still need to meet face to face,' you say.

Excuses, excuses from everyone!
Everyone blames pandemic 2020!
Well, all that is Covid history!

We all have a blame for it
Keep the circle of the planet
unbroken
Hope the lesson was learnt!

THIS DAY

A new-born dawn
Dresses the new day
In still silence
Giving my five senses
A full breakfast
Of praise and glory
On the path I walk
There is a breakfast of worms
For the choristers at dawn

MY LOCKDOWN in 2020

Wrote and completed *The Captive's Crown*
Wrote some Covid poetry
Created a lockdown video on *Their Journey* book
Browsed and discovered Steve Laube's Agency
Joined Association of Christian Writers
Reopened links with social media and Goodreads
Attempted traditional publishing
Attended Zoom birthdays for grands

Interacted with family in Nigeria
For tributes celebrating ECA @70!
Continued going to work once a week
Played table tennis in the evenings with hubby
Daughters work from home
Engaged in strolls
Attended family and prayer meetings on Zoom
Attended cell group meetings on Zoom

Husband turned seventy
Cake, pics and tasty Jollof rice
Iyan and rich okro and vegetable soup

From Tasty Woolwich for the day
Platinum birthday booklets arrive
Booklets posted to Nigeria,
Germany, UK, and USA
Attended two funerals on Zoom
Registered with old school associations

SODOM

I will destroy this city,
It is coloured in hate
It speaks discrimination
It feeds falsehood
It holds prejudice
It reeks of evil
It sings blasphemy
It breeds confusion
Between males and females
There is no fear of God
All are foolish
No one is good
except you, Abraham!
The blood of
virgins, orphans,
mothers and fathers
The homeless and
murder victims
cry out to me—
I will destroy Sodom!

Have mercy, Lord,
Save Sodom, I cry
For the sake of fifty?
I will
For forty-five or forty?
I will
For thirty-five or thirty?
I will
for twenty?
I will
For ten?
I will
Surely as surely
As I live
Sodom is able
To boast
Of ten good
people!
Surely!

Abraham stopped.
God waited and waited…
Interceding had ended.
Sodom was destroyed!

GO BACK AND STAY PUT!

Your anger
Where from?
You are so mad—
Or are you drunk?
Why run out
Of your house
Like one who is
Possessed or crazy
Your boundaries
Have been set
Your limits drawn
From creation

Now you come
To my home
Like a monster
With sea jaws
Devouring my loves
My family
All I have
Can't you see

This space
Can't contain
Both of us
You cry to me
For help
What can I do?

With sorrow
Upon me and
My loved ones
Upon our city
Now impoverished
You brought death
To visit us
Our wailings from
The horror of our loss

Your rebellion
Is your revenge
For provoking you
For persisting in
Those activities
That harm you
Our loss
Our sorrow and
Our death

Turn you
Into a monster
Running out of its hiding
And devouring
In its path
Land, trees, houses,
Fathers, mothers, children
Our souls and lives…

PLEASE STOP!

VOLCANO BREAFAST

What you have
Done, makes me
Throw up
Did you alter
The carbon
Content in my
Cup of tea?
It's too much!
It is too sweet
But it's harmful
To my health

Do you realise
My health matters
To your health?
If I throw up
Our home
Will be
Destroyed!
You might
Even lose

Your life
If you
Love carbon a lot

Make my tea
Using
Biodegradable
stuff
Remember we aren't
The only ones
In this home
AND
Our lives are
Entwined!

THE OCEAN'S PLEA

Hey! We like it clean here.
For years before you existed
This was a peaceful haven
Teeming with all kinds of amazing life
You came down here
You captured what you saw
You put your discoveries
In your documentaries
We liked that.

You studied our ways of life:
How we reproduce
How we live peacefully
How we fight
How we respect each other
How we contribute to life
How we adapt to life here
How we show love and care
You agree that we are intelligent—
Our ways mystify you
We liked your explorations

We assumed your keenness was
To help your fellow mankind

Why now do you harm us?
Why do you pollute our home
Why do you endanger our lives
You diminish our food
You foul the water
Now we are under pressure
Some of our neighbours
Are in extinction
What shall we tell our
Future generations?
What are all these plastics here,
Causing us stress?

This is no longer friendship
And you ask why we rebel
With floods destroying you!
What do you expect?
Until you show respect
For marine life and protect
Our neighbour species,
Until you filter your filth
Until you learn
Harmony and not harm

Until you learn
Respect not ruin
Until you learn
To save and not siphon
Until you learn
To keep and not kill
Until you learn
To protect and not plunder
Until you learn
Wisdom and not war
Until you learn
Peace and not poverty
Until you learn
Preservation and not pollution
Until you learn
To dream and not destroy

We will flood you
Flood your homes
Flood your property
Flood your family
Flood your loved ones
AND
Treat you as enemy!

KNIFE KILLERS

Another son dead!
His life at an end,
His loved ones crying
For the dying
Of their loved one lying
In a hearth
To buried in the earth
For his untimely death
The sorrow breaks their heart

What a waste to life!

FAITH –
GOD AND HIS CREATION,
BIBLE INSPIRATIONS,
BELIEF AND ENCOURAGEMENT

THE KING'S DAUGHTER

How do they know
That I am the daughter of the King of kings?
My Papa God!
The Creator of the universe!

As I walk along the road to school,
The trees have lined up both sides of the road
Deep bowls of garlands – pink, white confetti
The birds of the air chirp praises of greetings,
hailing me
The trees bow their boughs

Oh, look at those birds there!
They have left their breakfast of grub
and worms
They have abandoned their games
Chasing and playing hide and seek
They give me music
All along my school path as
I talk to my King

I acknowledge the buzz greetings
Of bees on shrubs along my path
The sun's morning rays kiss me
Good morning, Daughter of the King!

BLESSED BE YOUR NAME

YOU took Yesterday
Gave me Today
You took Last Year
Gave me This Year
YOU took my Maidenhood
Gave me Womanhood
YOU took my Spinsterhood
Gave me Wifehood
YOU took my Childhood
Gave me Motherhood
YOU took my Black Hair
Gave me White Hair
YOU took my Children
Gave me Grandchildren
YOU took my Death
Gave me Life

Blessed be Your Name
Blessed be Lord Jesus
Blessed be the Holy Spirit
Blessed be Papa God

I PRAISE YOU

I praise You,
You took Mother
I praise You
And my father
I praise You
Precious journeyed to Heaven
To meet You in 2015
I praise You
Elizabeth my sister
Whisked away
From my embrace in 2022
Just to heed Your calling
I praise You
Prostate Cancer came,
Brushing my spouse

I praise You,
Beautiful Vivian, my friend
Your chorister in church
Struck down in 2019 with
The lightning of cancer

I praise You
I am still Yours
I praise You
My lips and heart cry
I praise You
I know that all things
Work together
For my good
I praise You

FREEDOM IN CHRIST

Be open to God's Spirit
Enjoy freedom in Christ
Do not live in fear
The fear of change
The fear of the unknown
The fear of new ways and paths
The fear of new ideas and systems
The fear of anything else
Do not let fear rob you of
Enjoying the salvation of the Lord
The freedom in Christ

MY INVISIBLE FRIEND

I cannot see him or her,
For quite a very long while,
I was being wooed—
My spirit impressed this on my mind
Someone so desperately wants to be closer to me
I was conscious of this presence.

I had always wished I had a friend
Closer than a brother, closer than a sister,
Closer than a spouse
And closer than my earthly friends.
An intimate relationship,
Pure and not sinful
Despite being married to my spouse.

The Christian Bible says,
'Woe is the man that leaneth on man.'
No one is to be trusted

How I longed for someone I could trust,
Someone I could lean on

Pour out myself, my being, my whole soul and mind
Maybe this daily longing
Drew this presence to my awareness.

My longing was expressed in my dreams
I created daydreams
This friend that knew me in and out
Satisfied me in every way;
Could make me feel so loved,
So beautiful, and
Bring out the best in me;
Made me new, inspired the gifts in me
Made me be the best in the abilities
I thought I naturally possessed.

This friend has no flaws, no guile, deceit, or fault
This friend embodied passion, wisdom,
Knowledge, energy and limitless love.
Was it Aladdin's genie that invoked this?
The wish to have a friend out of this world,
But also in this world with me
Satisfying my every imagination, urge, need, desire,
My wants, longings, wishes, cravings and dreams?
I feel comfortable to think that this friend is
A *male and female combined.*

The Christian Bible put the notion in me
That a woman was made from a rib taken from a
man,
Who himself was breathed into his form
By our Almighty God
This makes me partly supernatural
This friend is 'Him'!

CARE YE NOT WE PERISH?

The storm in our life:
We could experience storms
in various degrees in every stage of life
Remember to call Lord Jesus into your boat
or to wake Him if it appears He is asleep
with a rebuke – "Care Ye not we perish?"
That wakes Him up!
With an outstretched hand He commands—
PEACE BE STILL!

The storm becomes still
and calm

PROCLAIMING THE GOOD NEWS!

We all love to hear good news
It brings excitement and joy and
in most cases could be life changing—
like in the cases of a new baby,
a new career,
a job promotion,
a long-expected healing
or even a new published book!

I bring you all the good news
of my new book, *The Captive's Crown*
Our Lord Jesus Himself had
asked his followers
to go and proclaim the
Good News of His resurrection
and that He was the way to the Father
through faith in Him,
our Lord Jesus.

This was going to be done by word of mouth
with the Holy Spirit's help.

In our generation, however,
I thank God
there are so many
communication channels.

It took angels, shepherds, a star,
the wise men, and John the Baptist
to proclaim the Good News
of the Messiah.

THE PEACE OF GOD

Toiling without stress is the blessing of peace
His blessings enrich, and add no sorrow,
the peace of God is all we need
He prepared us for the lives we each live,
He equipped us for the challenges of life.

Psalm 23 says, 'The Lord is my Shepherd,
I shall not lack'. Best of all,
He has given us the armour
to stand against the wiles of the enemy
through His Word
and so, we shall live and not die,
but declare the glory of God. Psalm 118:17.

Even if the world around you crashes,
God will give you His peace. Psalm 91.
The thoughts of Peace the Lord our God
has towards you
in *every* aspect of your life—
Let this give you all hope
PEACE of God that passeth all understanding

shall keep our hearts and minds
through Christ Jesus.
For I know the thoughts that I think toward you,
says Jehovah, thoughts of peace and not of evil,
to give you hope in your latter end.
Thank You, Papa God,
that the thoughts and plans You have for us
are for Peace and good, not evil.

Peace is a blessing in our lives.
Going to bed each night
without the fear of not waking up,
is peace.
God gives His beloved sleep.
Going out in the morning
to pursue your daily labour
without any fear
and arrive safely home
at the end of the day in one piece,
is the peace of God.

CREATIVITY

God's creation and creativity—
He created a magnificent world
in the midst of chaos! Like our Father,
we must continue to be creative
no matter the 'chaos'
we find ourselves in,
beauty will come out of ashes and
God's creation and creativity
would serve and achieve
its purpose on Earth

THE STEPS OF THE GOOD PERSON

God will direct you all the way, step by step
You don't audibly hear His directions
all the way
He just gives you the way to go and you trust
You know that whatever steps you take
They are right for you—
You believe and trust God.

Then plunge ahead like a blind bat
Every book I write is an unknown
Till it is finished and published.

Looking back at what I did
nineteen years ago
in leaving Nigeria to come to the UK,
I ask myself sometimes
if I am a risk taker?
Did I place my faith in luck or God then?
Was I aware of the quoted scripture
above then?

Certainly not as I do now!
I realise God loves people who take bold actions,
taking the plunge as long as…

This made me understand those who
are not of the Christian faith but
succeed abundantly all the same—
I know God makes the sun
to shine on everyone.

KEEP YOUR EYES UP!

When I look up
I see the glory of God:
The sky does not fall on my head
The clouds remain in place
The birds of the air are going about their business
The tree are mighty tall
They catch the morning breeze
They sway their branches
Their leaves rustle to the melody
They are proud of their new foliage
They have new adornments for the season
They burst with health toward the heavens

I am happy, filled with joy
The sky, clouds, hills, birds, planes—
Like David, I ask God
What is man that you should so pamper him
With your image, grace and salvation?

Then I look down like Peter
I see the havoc of man:

A dog walker has left a soiled path
Russia and Ukraine are in war
Food prices go up
Fuel prices go up
Houses are unaffordable
Rents are increased, but not salaries
Companies fold up

Family people, workers made redundant
Stress, depression arise
Teenagers grow wild
Vaping and smoking and drugs
Knife crime on the rise
Pupil exclusions on the rise
Single parenthood on the increase
Keep your eyes up—
Plead to Papa God

THE CLAY CAN TALK (Amos 3:7)

Papa God! You hear me,
I'm angry and disappointed
That is not a crime
No laws against that
Against such emotions
I'm not murmuring
In complaint or protest

You tell me Your ways
They aren't my ways
Your thousand years
Is my evening gone
Your breath is in my lungs
From dust, You made me
You numbered my days
Three score and ten years
Or a century and a score
You are God of all flesh

I am flesh and Your image but
I am not omnipotent

I am not omnipresent
I am not omniscient
I am not Alpha
I am not Omega
I cannot see You
I cannot hear You
Yet you give no sign
You dwell in silence's comfort

You are invisible
I am visible
You are spirit
I am human
You are heavenly
I am earthly
I haven't grumbled
Potter, can You help me?
It is Your clay talking!

SUNDAY SERVICE

Let your life please the Lord!

I was there waiting—
I knew what I was waiting for.
I had been sifting the words
Words from the pastor's mouth
Words about visiting
Words about Western End
Words about fools and horses
Words about belly laugh
Words that shared gratitude
Gratitude to God

There was no racism
There were no swear words
There was no sexy language
At Western End
Then the words changed
How does one know right?
Buying an expensive car?
Dressing less than modest?

Building more than two houses?
Enjoying more than two bottles of wine?
What does the Bible say?
Does the Bible say what is right?

I stopped sifting words.
The meat had begun to fall
What I had been waiting for
My waiting was over.
The meat came in deep bowls,
The Bible says, Romans 8:12,
Be bold, be courageous,
Do not compromise God's words.
Paul did not
I am called not to
I live in a world
A world of compromises
Of lukewarm attitudes
To the things of God
God says, 'Be at peace with all men
As far as you can.'

I get lots of meat
It might take time a while
A while to digest the meat
The meat will last me

The meat will take me
Take me through the week
Till the next Sunday
To hear the Word of God
The meat of my God
For my soul

FROM THE CROSS

This burden is so heavy
Crushing my sore bent back
How will I last it out?
A day being like years on end
I don't pray you stand here
You see me on this cross
Your imaginations
Your thoughts
Your dreams
Your senses
Can't fathom this cross
I bear

It's the second day
I'm still alive
Still alive to reason
If He helped me this far
To endure the burden
From this cross I bear
Will He see me through?
Will this cross end soon?

Will this pain see its termination?
Will this heart know freedom and peace?
His Word – Joy, comes in the morning
I wait in hope

It's the third day
In the dark valley
The darkness is pitch black
The heaviness numbs me
Devoid of any weight
Where is the peace and freedom?
My soul cries out—
How have I endured two days?
Which felt like forever from the cross of
Despondence, despair, depression, disease
Failure, fatigue, frailty, fear
Barrenness, brokenness, bitterness
and bereavement

Where are You, Lord?

I hear You whisper:
My grace is sufficient for you
I carry the cross
I bear the burden
I comfort you with My Holy Spirit

I give you peace not as the world
I give you My joy for strength
I have not given you a spirit of fear
I sent My Word to heal you and give you life
I show you Love
I gave you My name to defend you
I sent My Son for your hope in eternity

Thank You Lord for yesterday, now and today
Thank You for strength, peace and joy
Thank You for mercy, favour and love
Thank You, my Papa God,
You Grace is enough
In any situation
Your gift of eternity
Gives me hope

HOLY SPIRIT

Holy Spirit or Holy Ghost
You are one and the same
You obeyed the Son – Lord Jesus
You kept your promise
To descend forty days on Earth
After the Son's ascension to Heaven
To dwell in fellow believers

A lot is said about you—
You are the power of God
You are the third part of the Trinity
You can be grieved
You dwell in Christ believers
You are Helper, Inspirer, Comforter,
Encourager, Reminder, Enabler
You are Fire, Wind, Water
You are Life and so much more!

As I think of You
I am consciously reminded
You want to be much more

In relationship with me
To know me in and out
Is your invisible nature a deterrent?
Deterring me from your presence?
Encourage me to acknowledge You
With all my thinking faculty
In my mortal being
To Your presence in me
Remind me, enable me, inspire me,
Through fire, wind, and water
To enjoy Your presence
in me

HEAVEN

Thank You, Papa God
For this privilege
To share thoughts of Heaven
Your place of abode
Your throne, our Creator
Your mercy seat
A place of mystery
That veils your mysteriousness
A place You harvest
As mankind's goal
A place of final rest
The destination for man's soul

I love that Heaven
Reconciles our loved ones
To us – Parents, Grandparents,
Siblings and Family

Heaven – a home for all homes
A palace with rooms
Marking out each person's name

A magnificent place
No human mind can fathom
It's beyond human imagination
A place only for departed souls
From Planet Earth

HAVE FAITH

Stop your wasting time
Asking God questions
He depends on your faith

Stop your waiting impatiently
Expecting God's solutions
He responds to your faith

Stop your blaming
Expecting God's sympathy
He depends on your faith

Stop your self-deception
Leaning not on God's strength
He responds to your faith

Stop your being stingy to charity
Denying the promises of God
He responds only to your faith

Stop your rejecting the Word
Engaging ungodly beliefs
He depends on your faith

Stop your faithlessness
Shutting God out of your life
He depends on your faith

Stop your ignoring the Holy Spirit
Thinking and feeding the flesh
He responds to your faith

Stop fighting your destiny
Not understanding God's plan
He responds to your faith

Stop your comparing to others
God made everyone unique
He responds to your faith

Stop your fears
It shows not trusting God
He depends on your faith

Stop trying to understand God
Try knowing God
He depends on your faith

Stir your faith up
Pray and hope in God
Papa God will use faith and bless you.

WHY DIDN'T YOU ASK HIM

Peter! You got named *Rock*
for your boldness—
Why didn't you ask Him
what you'd do in Heaven?

Andrew and John! Sons of Zebedee
You got named *Boanerges* – Sons of Thunder
Why didn't you ask Him
about your dead ancestors
if they can see you from Heaven?

James! You were the Lord's brother
He was your mother's son
Surely you could have asked Him
what happened on Resurrection Sunday?

Mary! You were His mum—
Chosen for your favour with God
You saw Him return from the wilderness
Why didn't you ask Him to ask Papa God
to give people the power to resist the devil?

MY TIME WITH YOU

I am alone here,
All quiet and still
Even the wind and trees
Time to be still—
Keep quiet and still
Before my Papa God

It's a new day,
My mind isn't still
Lots of things there
Like a cooking pot
Cooking summer's heat
Bites from the sand flies as
Their bodies graze mine
My daughters are travelling,
Holidaying to Turkey but
In bed they sleep still—
Will they be late?
Miss their Turkey flight?
Read Job's first two chapters,
The devil's so wicked

My mind's bubbling still
Cooking up a lot of stuff
But You, Papa God
Wait for me still—
Your presence is still
Waiting for my mind
To be very still
You calmed the storms,
Calm my mind, Papa
Command it to stay still

In Your presence
The trees are still
The wind is still
I see my Bible
It's time to listen
Like You have listened
To my rambling mind
I pick my Bible
I listen to You
In Job three and four

ALL LIFE IS A CANDLE

All life is a candle
Burning longer
Burning shorter
Burning faster
Burning slower

All life is a candle
It begins strong
It stays young
It stays long
It's time to sow
But what to sow?
Tears or laughter to sow?

Al life is a candle
It burns to its middle
Faster, slower – depends,
Constructive or destructive thoughts?
Healthy or unhealthy lifestyle?
Forgiveness or unforgiveness?
Peace or conflict?

All life is a candle
It reaches its end
In seconds, minutes, hours
In days, weeks, months
In years, decades, seasons
In jubilees, platinums, octagons
In God's timing

All life is a candle
While it lasts
Keep to God's way
Focus on His Word
It transforms
It brings joy and strength
It brings blessings
It is God's power on Earth
To lead to life eternal

INSPIRED BY JOB 9 ABOUT GOD

He is all powerful—
No one can argue with Him
No one can answer His question
No one sees Him
No one knows when He comes in
Or when He goes out
He comes in and takes what He wants
No one can stop Him

He moves mountains
He causes them to vomit lava
He moves the Earth's boundary
Till they tremble and quake
He does things without warning
He creates new days
None is the same
He creates beings in their millions
And no one is duplicated

He sends his angels to do His will
He gives humans their talent

He gives them wisdom
He gives them power
He gives them fortune
He opens and closes wombs
He opens and closes doors of favours
He provides and shuts opportunities
He breathes life and death

He actively and passively hears prayers
He answers or withdraws requests to prayers
All according to His will
He searches the depths of human hearts
He sees what they really are
He scans their thoughts
He is able to decipher their motives
His eyes, like lenses, magnify their secret deeds
His ears, like detectors, hear unspoken words
and silent thoughts

Humans cannot understand the evil
The injustice in the world or
The extent of wickedness in humans displayed
In their steady corruption
Inconsideration, thoughtlessness, selfishness
Power drunkenness, bestial natures or
Wars, attacks and physical combats

That maim, devastate and ruin humans
and their environment

God is omnipresent
Yet all these happen on Earth
We will know when we meet Him
Face to face, someday
Then the light of reason and understanding
Will ignite our wisdom
and judgement

PRAISE

It is powerful
It is prayer
It is promising
It is personal
It is pleasure
It is pleasant
It is practical
It is peaceful
It is pulling

It is awesome
It is angelic
It is affection
It is adorable
It is accomplishment
It is absolute
It is acknowledgement
It is advantageous
It is afflatus

It is worship

It is wealth

It is wonderful

It is warmth

It is wholesome

It is welfare

It is wellbeing

It is willingness

It is witnessing

OUR GOD

God of miracles
God of the impossible
You created humans from the dust
You multiplied few loaves of bread to feed thousands
You hold the seasons and the planets
You took Enoch in flesh to Heaven
You raised Lazarus to life after three days
You triumphed over death
You let water out of a rock in the desert
You parted the Red Sea
You rained manna from Heaven
You closed the lion's mouth and saved Daniel
You didn't let the fire burn
You sent a whale to save Jonah
You delivered Israel from Egypt
You restored Job's health and wealth
You healed the blind, crippled, lepers and the deaf
and dumb
You made the universe from Your Word
You made the Jericho walls fall
You made David, the shepherd boy, king

You made Joseph, the slave, prime minister
You made Esther, a common girl, queen
You made man in Your image
You make impossible possible
You saved Moses from the Nile, desert and Pharaoh
You saved Noah and his family from the flood
You gave Solomon divine wisdom
You gave Job extraordinary patience
You gave Samson supernatural strength
You gave Mary, the maiden, distinguished favour
You gave Abraham uncommon faith
You gave Joshua unusual might
You gave Elijah unusual vision
You gave Isaac to aged Abraham and Sarah
You gave John the Baptist to aged Zechariah and
barren Elizabeth
You gave Gideon valour
You gave the world salvation
You gave us eternal life

DEVIL IN MY CUP OF TEA

Look who's here this morning!
What here are you doing,
uninvited? Of course, you say nothing
But you always do something
I hear your subtle whispering
luring me with your tempting,
toying with my faith. Trying
and luring me to doubting.

Get thee behind me, devil!
Your thoughts are so evil
I am for God's will
You will make me ill
My life in God's wheel,
gets me on my heel,
where you cannot kill
God's plan for me, till
I have accomplished His will.

HAIKU PRAYER

My dear Papa God
Thanks for my inspiration
Bless all my writings

HAIKU PRAISE

Dearest awesome God
I sit in my living room
Your blessings abound

HAIKU GRATITUDE

I am sixty-four
Thank you for my family
I am full of joy

SORTED (inspired from Revelation)

Before the beginning,
it started in God's omniscient mind—
creation had been created.
Pride, the enemy of God,
incubated evil.
Its fruits of sin and death
fell as seeds to mankind,
corrupting all flesh and
dooming mankind
to eternal damnation
and destruction.

Where is salvation
from an omnibenevolent Father?
The enemy gloats
in victory of absolute power
in hope of being God.
Eager to fulfil plans
to punish mankind
as revenge for his ousting
from Eden Garden

from the paradise
of complete bliss and perfection
from a glory never to grasp

He hears God asking:
who will go below
and get crushed
by the weight of
mankind's sin?
Who is worthy?
There is silence
in all Heaven
never heard before
poignant with dread
no one dares breathe.

The enemy gloats,
perceiving a foreshadow
of his own glory
then the silence
is broken
with the sound of
"Here I am. Send me!"

A saviour is born,
mankind is redeemed

from eternal doom
the enemy is defeated
death is conquered
the task is done
victory is accomplished.

It pleased
the Father
to crush
His son
to save
mankind

Amen.

JOSEPH'S DREAM

When life happens
You think of your dreams
Those dreams of splendour
Inspired by magnificent desires
Great goals to achieve that
Overcome limitations,
And challenges.
And rising to the ladder top
Of glory and shining down
On all who are below,
Like a king in majesty

When life comes in the way
What can sway it away
Who can tell it to go away
It makes family shun your dreams
They hate you for the light they see in you
They despise that you are favoured
They are fearful you are a rising star
Those closest to you are jealous
They ponder and wonder and shudder

Boiling in hateful stews
That kill all filial bonds of love
You see yourself as a rainbow in the sky,
Dressed in robes of many dazzling colours
You were being singled out over others
You have enjoyed unique favour
That ignited a hidden fire
Soon the flames blaze around you
The heat wakes you
It's no dream
You are in a pit
Dark, steep, deep, and gloomy
Your cries elicit hateful laughter

You are not a dreamer
You are a slave
In a foreign land
Those dreams, were they lies?
Now you are a servant
It doesn't get better
You are a prisoner
You stop counting the rolling years
Your family is a dream
Your life in Canaan is a dream
You believe it's all a nightmare
You will wake up from

You become a dream interpreter—
What an irony

Your dreams landed you in prison
It was a dream that freed you from prison
It was a dream that shot you up
To the position of prime minister
In Egypt
It was a dream that brought reconciliation
With your Canaan family
It was a dream that made you a saviour
Of kingdoms

GOD'S WINTER

The cold
breath of our
Lord comes blasting
this time to warm our hearts.

Every winter season, every year,
our world here is wrapped in icy sheets, dripping.
Naked trees patiently wait for their new season.
The world prospers in peace and festivity at this
time—
in expectation of the Lord's lamb and Saviour,
the bringer of our hope and joy
God's winter ushers in the warmth of love.

The heat of the fireplace and rekindled fire in our
hearts
Thawing away all griefs and sorrows as hearty meals
and gifts are shared
The new season springs out the beauty of
dazzling wraps, tinsel, and light.
The merriment of songs sung in the air and

our hearts receive the exchange of love,
from fellowship and unity of family, friends,
colleagues, neighbours and brethren.

The family feasts on the twenty-fifth celebrate
the newborn babe ushered into our world,
to save our lives and to rekindle love,
to share blessings of kindness,
to spread true happiness,
to change old ways,
rebirth ourselves
in new lives of
Salvation.

ABRAHAM

Adonai!
You are God, but my friend
In dreams, I saw You
You told me things only I knew
You drew close to my heart and spirit
You groomed my trust
You fed my hope with faith
You whispered promises of love.

You trained my inner man with strength,
You prepared my mind with resolve like steel
You gifted me with the most beautiful woman
You surrounded me with favour all around me
Whatever I touched prospered
In visions, You introduced yourself
Adonai, my God and Master.

Finally, You called me,
I followed you to the new home.
There, You blessed me beyond imagination:
You promised me an heir of Promise!

You brought me and mine into an everlasting
covenant
You blessed my unborn generations
You showered me with blessings of the morning
You imbued the afternoon blessings over me
You commanded the blessings of the evening to
shroud me
At night, You blessed my soul with Your visitation.

You are my best friend,
I will always serve You with my faith!
You will always be my vision, day and night
I will always do Your bidding
I promised You and have not faulted
You have tested me severally and I have surprised
You
Yet my loins remained unaffected by all Your
blessings—
You always have Your reasons.

I waited for fifty years, not complaining once
The son of promise came, but today, what did you
s*ay?*
Did I hear You well – to offer my only seed as
sacrifice?

Another test?
I will not fail You or break my promise.

I know You don't believe in human sacrifice
I know You won't break the promise You made to me
I know You want me to have complete faith in You

TAKE my Isaac!

Surely, You know what You are doing—
Alas! You stayed my hand!

Now You applaud me with – Father of Faith!

YAHWEH

He – the Omnipresent God
Sees through our eyes
Dazzles with our vision
Works through our minds
Meddles with our thoughts
Creates through our hands
Fiddles with our creation
Moulds through our imagination
Springs with our revelation and
Science comes forth
Emerging with technology
Like dust and ribs
Like the rainbow

He – the Omnipotent God
Creates with words
What science can't fathom
Without the big bang theory
Performs miracles
That technology can't decode
Like the creation in six days

Like the red sea parting
Like the rubble of the Jericho walls
Like the birth of Your Son
Like the earthly life of Your Son
Like the death of Your Son
Like the resurrection of Your Son

Reels out numbers mentally
Like the number of seashore sand
Like the number of head hair
Like the number of stars
Like walking on water
Like unmuting the deaf
Like opening sight to the blind
Like enabling the lame
Like transforming impossible to possible
Fought victoriously without an army
Fed five thousand with five sandwiches
Changed era of civilizations
Through death
Through shorter life spans
Through language
Through a forty day and night flood
Through diversity and religion
Through planned plagues and viruses
Through natural disasters

Through science and technology
Through the power in Jesus Christ's name
Through the blood of Jesus

He – the Omniscient God
Puzzles the brains of scientific geniuses
Defies their reasoning
Undermines their theories
Baffles their intelligence
Mocks their wisdom
Dislodges their assumptions
Deflates their ballooned powers
Mystifies their understanding
Confuses their solutions
Perplexes their musings
Dissatisfies their curiosity
Unwinds their ramblings
Tampers with their findings
Teases with their dissertations
Toys with their notions
Faults their knowledge
Their concept of the Trinity

He – the Almighty Abba God
Blows their feathered confidence
Baffles their curiosity

Unnerves their conclusions
Displays their limitations
Stirs their confusion
Invokes their philosophy
Inspires their quests
Unquenches their thirst
Expands their motivation
Expends their energies
Conquers their conquests
Dissipates their strengths
Authors their talents
Probes their quests
With their carnal minds
As man battles man
To disprove the claims of God
To deny His existence
To pervert His art
To disqualify His abilities
To refute His origins
To disclaim His blessings
To forsake His ways
To destroy His credibility
To mislead generations of mankind
With their poison of
Hatred and sin of unbelief

He – Jesus, God personified in miracle and marvel

He – God of Revelation

He – God of Redemption

He – Father, Son and Holy Spirit

He – Omnibenevolent God

He – The Creator of life and all

He – God of Heaven and Earth

He – Faithful, Holy God

He – God of Love

He – God of Glory

He – God of Salvation

He – Kings of kings, resurrected King

He – Lord of lords, Lord over death

He – Crown of Victory

He – God of Transcendence and Immanency

He – God of Goodness

He – God of Grace and Graciousness

He – God of wisdom

He – God of Truth

He – God of Praise

He – God of Mercy

He – God of Compassion

He – God of All and Everything

Your breath in every man
Your favour in Your pleasure

Your creation in Your will
Your Holy Spirit is invisible
Tremendously mighty
In stillness, power, and calm
The light of the soul
Enshrouded in Your desire
You hold mystery in your hands
You awe man with Your laughter
Like a mother coos to her amused infant
You keep the mystery of You
Unveiled and unlocked
Till time in eternity with You

AMEN

BREATHE IN MY DIRECTION

I have a different way
Your ways are not mine

It's okay to be discouraged
It's okay to be disjointed
It's okay to feel disappointed
It's okay to feel forsaken
It's okay to be angry

It's okay when I don't
sing for joy
It's okay to ask You why
It's okay to feel empty
It's okay to feel anguish

You brought Seth
When there was no
Cain and Abel
You brought the Holy Spirit
When you took Jesus

Let me understand You—
Breathe in my direction,
Then I can see
With understanding
What you are doing
And why you do it

A GOOD SEED

Rich, fertile
Yielding fruits
Good, healthy
Overflowing
Its capacity
Like abundance
Of fish
Breaking nets

Invisible, powerful
Inside of you
Waiting to bud
The power
Of Faith
Yielding to you
Impossibilities become
Possible
Replacing disbelief
With belief
Receiving promises
In faith

Yielding an
Explosion of
God's
Supernatural blessings

Quit the
Grounds of worry
Of doubt, fear
And faithlessness
A fatal mix
With Faith
Yielding defeat
Loss and no profit

Keep the Faith
Child of the
Most High
God!

ADVENT

A season of hope
A feeling of hope
A time of rebirth
An increase of faith
A recognition of a new season
An expectation of receiving
A demonstration of sharing
An awareness of God's reality
An exercise of authority
A release of festivity
A call to reconciliation
An illustration of revelation
A miracle in action
An agreement to salvation

A gift of salvation
An outpouring of God's glory
An indication of victory
A show of open-heartedness
A shift from worldliness
A reminder of choice and justice

An atmosphere of peace
A promise fulfilled
A change of heart
An obedience performed
A step up to grace
A birth of freedom
A display of power
A celebration of love
A focus on Jesus Christ

CHRISTIANITY IS NOT EASY

Christ is Love.
You follow Christ
You have to become like Him
You love all people
For the good of humanity

Love your enemies
Who wish you evil
Love annoying people
In their habits and lifestyle
Love strangers
You meet in everyday life
Love Christian-haters
Who see your faith as fake
Love your neighbours
Who scream your walls down
Love those pet owners
Whose pets mess your space
Love the authorities
Who oppress you
Love your in-laws

Who demean you
Love friends and family
Who wish your downfall
Love people of other faiths
Who persecute you

HUMANITY –
PEOPLE,
THEIR LIVES
AND EXPERIENCES

LAND FLOWING WITH MILK
AND HONEY

It was like living the hopeless life
of the Jews in Egypt
I had remained devoted to God.
When a mass of believers are together
in their pain,
their faith gives a divine strength to hope
until God provides a way out.
I had continued writing and
continued my job as a teacher even
when unpaid.

Like God heard the cries of His people,
mine was also heard.
God sent a lady to remind me of
my birth land
and advised me to relocate to UK
to teach!

It sounded preposterous.
My manuscripts followed me,

the way Moses carried his writings
of their lives in Egypt over to Canaan.
I never thought my writings would
ever get published!
It is amazing that people read our books
and see God's glory but never imagine
the fire we have passed through
or are passing through!

In this land of Milk and Honey
the Lord has brought me
may my writings continue
to help people see God's plan
for their lives
and increase their knowledge
of God.

Amen.

THE WIND

Letting my thoughts fly anywhere
to no purposeful destination
in subject matter is amazing.
There is no stopping—
just like the invisible wind
freely blowing in any direction.
My mind – is it empty?
What is in there?

There is no time to pause or think—
my thoughts, like the wind, are
just blowing whither they want,
not caring about rubbish,
mistakes, common sense or not,
beauty or not – or like the chaos

Well, just as the wind carries up dust particles,
anything in its wake,
so go my thoughts, picking up anything
that my mind throws at them
The wind gets fast, busy, cold or even hot

and sometimes even dangerous.
I have felt the teeth of the wind
on my skin and inside my nose—
These were not pleasant.
Or still and absent?
I felt hot and uncomfortable.
I remember times
the wind was beautiful to feel
on my entire body.

I thought then
of Abba, my Father in Heaven,
and blew him invisible kisses
for sending such feelings of love from the wind
caressing my entire being and
making my soul at one with Him.
At that moment,
there was definitely satisfaction,
contentment, peace and
the feeling to fly and be carried away
or to ride with the wind to
wherever it would take me!

IT'S NOT OVER

You took from me hope
After bringing me this far
You took my hope
Not finding what you said

You took hope from me
When my dream died
You took my hope
With your power

You took my hope
Not seeing your mercy
You took my hope
My goals did die
You took my hope
When you gave up on me

You took my hope
But it is not over
I still have a will
It is not over

My spirit is not crushed
It is not over
I can dream again
It is not over

I can create new goals
It is not over
I live in Faith

CHINWE

It's her birthday anniversary—
Celebrating the third year of life
For my fourth granddaughter
I travel to Colchester,
Two years I last saw her!
A fair, pretty quiet one
Becoming lively when her sister
Returns from school

I muse on my thoughts on the journey
What will she be like—
After this Covid while?
Still pretty quiet?
Still keeping a smile?
Would she squeak with pleasure
If I throw her up?

Would the gifts I bring her
Light up her face
Stir up giggles and
Twinkles in her eyes?

Or will she just take a peek
Throw it over the side?
When I get there,
I will know!
Right now,
I don't know.

AGE

I wake up and
I am six – ty – four – years – old!
All of a sudden
I can't remember the previous decades
I realise that I've gone past half way.
I don't panic but
I am angry—
I want to have my powers back:
nimble limbs to stand for long
to carry my weight
while I'm ignorant of time
sharp eyes to read aidless
to carry my sight
while I'm ignorant of time
dark, thick hair to adorn my head
to give me beauty and grace
while I'm ignorant of time

I look round my home,
I see all the evidence of my age and time
through the photographs all over my home

keeping track of the decades gone by
refreshing my memories of the ages gone by
I look forward in pride
and feel I can make a hundred in future

My anger fizzles out like breath on a wintry day
as the people I regard as family
look at me with smiles of love and appreciation
I look at me, too, from the truthful pictures—
they speak of my gaining weight
they point at what I can't grasp from time
they show the additions to my generation
they exhibit the work of my creativity

I no longer panic
I am not angry anymore
I have my powers still:
poetry and prose published
in fictions of faith and fantasy
motherhood to two generations
I have my powers still—
just in different dimensions

PAPER

The writer's canvas
Begins a blank slate
Devoid of a single letter
Like a black cloud
Without a ray of light
Then comes inspiration
From the author of the Word
The Giver of all inspiration—
Letters, words, phrases
Clauses and sentences
Multiply into paragraphs
That swell the chapters
From the first to the last
The beginning to the end
Digital paper
Electric paper
Reader's eyes gobble
Food for revelation

You receive everything, anything
From everyone, anyone

You submit to anybody, everybody
Like a sheep for sacrifice
Like me, you are nameless till named:
Wallpaper, wrapping paper, toilet paper, paper back
Idle till made busy:
Exams, excerpts, essays, art...
Like me, you have a life span and destination
Abrupt or long lived
To the library?
To the bin?
To the shredder?
Yet, you are so important
So valuable
To all mankind
Without you, ignorance and illiteracy
Will abound
Without you, where will be God's Word?
Without you, where will art be?
Where will my creativity be?
How can we be a blessing?

Lord, I bless You
For paper!

GREY HAIR

You say
It is a crown of splendour
It is attained in righteousness
It is the wisdom for the aged
It is length of days

You remind us that grey hair
Sets apart youth from elderly
Demarcates foolishness from maturity
Make a boundary
Between the age groups

Grey hairs have lived life
To decades flowing closer to a century
Bringing forth fruit
From loins of generations
To populate Earth

Grey hair – a blessing
A thing of beauty and pride
Not guilt, shame, or regret

It may sprout early, prematurely on
Heads of youths
Be not confused
Hereditary grey hairs
Belongs to all, but
Grey hairs sprout distinctively
On my head

Why do I shroud in shame?
I should be grateful.
Thank You, Papa God,
For Grey Hairs

MUSIC

Would I ever have known
The blessings without ears to hear
What good to see the new babe
But not hear its first cry
Its suckling and guzzling at feeding

Could I ever have imagined
The outburst of joy
To hear you are engaged
How long had I waited!
Or to hear you passed your exams
Or the ecstasy of news
Announcing the new arrival of a babe
Or the relief of hearing
You passed your driving test
Or healed from a plague

Would I ever have thought that
From nature my soul you bless
Through the sense of my ears
I hear your creations awake with dawn

Chirping, hooting, greeting
The trees are listening too
At their cue from the breeze
I will hear their worship and chatter
Muttering as they caress and play
Dancing to the music in the air

Could I have ever felt
The pleasure of belly laughter
That nourishes the soul
To hear comedians at their muse, folly, and art
Or hearing the amusing ironies of life
The blessings at celebrations
Of life, achievement, birth, and death
Never would I have felt the
Uplifting of my soul in church
Worshipping, praising, singing hymns
To Papa God

Would I ever have received
The knowledge, peace, comfort
Wisdom, counsel, from Your Word
Your Word given in scriptures
Is the music for my whole being
Is the pleasant sound of instruction
To direct my path to you

To instruct me in righteousness
To guide me from stumbling
To protect me from evil
To lead me to achieve Heaven

Could I have ever experienced
Hearing the beauty of silence
To hear its music of peace
To my soul
Its music of solace
Enveloping my being
Its music of creativity
Engulfing me in flames of words
Entrenching me in a world of fantasy
Expanding my horizon from the physical
To the realms of make-believe
In deep reflection, meditation, and inspiration
At the table You set daily before me
Each moment of my life

Would I finally hear
The choir of Heaven someday
The ecstasy, awe, and glory
Beyond any human comprehension in flesh
Beyond mortal imagination or reasoning
Even the music of lightning, thunder, and fire

Wind, rain, snow, sea, and rocks or
The most alluring, sweetest sounds in creation
Still no human like me can imagine that time
In spirit and mind, body or soul
Till one day I be part of the celestial choir

WORK DONE

How the heart leaps like a grasshopper
In excitement and expectation
In time to the clock's tick
Journeying to the exact hour
Exact minute, exact second
It's 3pm – time to clock out
Time to breathe a sigh
Time to feel relieved
Time to pick coat and bag
Time to catch bus 469
It comes and buzzes round
Stopping to pick, stopping to drop
Finally, I drop
Exhausted but elated

LAST DAY 29/07/2022

Last day of school today
All happy and excited this day
Except one.
All discussing holiday
Except one.
This last day
Brings the summer holidays
Time for leisure and play
Time to sleep all day

Staff wear relief on their faces
Pupils flash smiles on their faces
Except one with a sad face
He has always dreaded this day
Like a plague that blights the day
His best days are the school days
His place of haven shifts on this day
He's going to be shut away
From a summer of play
From the care and support
The nourishment from each school day

For this one, it will be aches
From child labour all day
Denial of love and care all day
Exposure to violence and abuse all day
Home life is prison all day
This one will hibernate
Till the end of the holidays
And awake at resumption day

FRANCIS, OUR FIRSTBORN

Papa God sent us a son
To open my womb
An answer to a heart's prayer
Tall, fair, spitting image of my love
I learnt to nurse and nurture
My first of fruits
Today, you are a man after God's heart,
You have found your better half—
A woman of virtue and strength
Now, you are a husband and a dad
You built a nest around God's Word
You honoured your parents' words

So proud of you always.
This day, you mark the last rung
On the third floor of life's ladder,
Monday nineteenth, in the year 2022,
A year away from another milestone
Father of three, receive our gift of blessings
Medical physician, your hands are blessed

May your righteous path of life,
Shine brighter and brighter to a perfect life
From God, receive uncommon favour
Receive increased grace from God
Your new age and family are blessed
With abundant blessings.
Your heart's desires,
Your growth in grace, favour, and spirit in God
Are our prayers for you now and always

This day, I lift you in prayer to my
Papa God, who never fails me.
Your children will make you proud
Your wife will be
God's best gift to you.
Amen.

LIFE CAN BE TOO SHORT

20 or less for some
30 or 40 for some
50 or 60 for some
66 for my Liz
33 for Him

Do not keep grudges
Spit it out
Life is too short

Do not keep malice
Break its chain
Life is too short

Do not keep unforgiveness
Kick it away
Life is too short

Do not hate
Tear it off
Life is too short

Do not quarrel

Back out

Life is too short

WILL YOU SAVE THEM?

In lessons, the phone pops out
Strongly defying school rules
It glues itself to their eager fingers
It lures them with friendly smiles
It tempts them with rude apparitions
It gives promises of unrealistic fame
It stuffs their ears with swear raps

Foul language overtakes theirs
Forbidden thoughts slitter out
Right into teenage hearts,
Turning them into school bullies
As they hurl, fling, and
Spread wickedness.

It steals their achievement
They are robed and rewarded with
Empty goals
An unfulfilled future awaits them
Disgruntled youths, like bats,
Are neither here nor there – misfits.

Sometimes, just only sometimes,
A glimpse of their true hearts
Peep out from the dark, heavy shadow
Of their oppressor.

Will you save them?

BEING GOD FOR A SECOND

I sit on God's cosy chair in heaven,
the earth beneath me
like a regular football
my feet are planted firmly
on the grounds of the universe

The world before me
is a screen
like a huge faced TV.
The whole of creation before me
like different channels
I just have a second in time
but much more in Heaven time
to indulge my whims

I peep at the thoughts of my husband
like a private spy
searching the recesses of his mind—
tea and cake there.
I dig further
and unearth all his hidden secrets

I smile – still craves for God's wisdom
and wealth

Next I peep into the life shelves
of each child of mine
like a peeping tom
I go through each one in fascination
I smile – all are about the
bustle of life
to succeed, survive, and strive in strength
all is well there

I change my focus
like one with a remote
I toss between two choices:
bask in creation's beauty or
hearken to a zillion cries
for divine intervention
I frown with heartache
I stick out my Stop Finger
like a magic wand
at the continents, commanding,
STOP THE GREED, CORRUPTION,
SELFISHNESS, WARS,
VIOLENCE, TREACHERY,
RUTHLESSNESS AND EVIL

Not much done with the finger
my anger wells up to boiling point
I stick out my Destroy Finger
but I am restrained
and reminded—
patience, not destruction
love, not hatred
life, not death

I see the rainbow
and remember
I see the Son
and understand
I rouse from
my dream.
To be God
is not
easy!

FOR A CHANGE

Say hi to yourself
Look closely at yourself
Observe closely
How unique you are
How wonderfully made you are
You might see freckles
Or scars and scabs
And dimples and pimples
Even moles and age spots
Yes! That is beautiful.

Others might see
Your protrusions or
Compare you to themselves
And find shortcomings
Find imperfections
That is to them!
Yes! Remember
You are you
You are not them
They are not you

For a change
Look at yourself
Observe yourself closely
See how unique you are
Say to yourself
I am wonderfully made
I am God's image
I am uniquely made
I am specially talented
I am God's wisdom
I am God's masterpiece
For a change
Say hi to yourself
Say you are able
Say you can
Say praises to yourself
Say good things to yourself
Yes! You are not self-conceited

For a change
Smile to yourself
Be patient with you
Be kind to yourself
Be loving to you

For a change
Say well done to yourself
For all your achievements today
You did not achieve all today's goals
You forgot some things to do
You made some mistakes today
You broke your promise today
Yes! You have not let God down

For a change
Acknowledge the one who counts – you
Accept your abilities
Rejoice at your achievements today
Praise your doings today
For a change
Give to yourself with generosity
Treat yourself with love
Be pleased with yourself
Be satisfied with your life
See your life as an opportunity
To appreciate you

For a change
Be grateful for you.

TIME

Time is a teacher
You learn patience, endurance
And resilience in the school of life

Time is a revealer
You learn knowledge, new truths
And revelation in the school of life

Time is patient
You learn to wait
And hope in the school of life

Time is an instructor
You learn realities
And realisations in the school of life

Time is a clock
You learn pacing and punctuality
And planning in the school of life

TURN BY TURN

Days, weeks and months go
Turn by turn in years
Spring, summer, autumn and winter go
Turn by turn in season
Seconds, minutes and hours go
Turn by turn in time
One, two, three and four go
Turn by turn in number
Rain, wind and sun go
Turn by turn in weather

Hot, warm and cold go
Turn by turn in temperature
Birth and death go
Turn by turn in life
Babyhood, childhood, teenhood and adulthood go
Turn by turn in maturity
Beginning, middle and end go
Turn by turn in a circle
Father, mother and children go
Turn by turn in the family

Morning, afternoon, evening and night go
Turn by turn in moments
Yesterday, today, tomorrow go
Turn by turn in the future
Good, better and best go
Turn by turn in quality
Kindness and respect go
Turn in turn in reciprocation
Honesty and diligence go
Turn in turn in achievement
Patience and perseverance go
Turn in turn in success

Trust and hope in God go
Turn in turn in Faith
Faith in God
Gives salvation

HOW LONG

You were born in chains
Of oppression, outrage, overworked, and
Overpowered
You couldn't afford to dream
Of luxury, life, laughter and longevity
You saw no hopeful future
Of your generations daring to dream
Your bent back in servitude
Of begging, borrowing in bitter bitterness

How long will deceit reign
From those who govern over you?
How is the anthem sung
From the lips of hungry people?
How can you spout patriotism
To treacherous hearts sown in corruption?
How can you see Right
From eyes blinded with gross injustice?

AUGUSTUS, OUR SECOND BORN

My second born child
His birth face fooled the family—
Dad or grandad looks?
Dimpled cheeks
Banana yellowed skin
Escaped the death jaws of jaundice

My second boy
Born with big bulgy eyes
Just like my father's and
Deserving his name – Augustus
Took my complexion

My second babe
Escaping the novice hands and
Benefitting from experienced maternal skills
Nurtured fully with maternal milk
Schooled in Kings' College, Lagos
Now, you are a king!

My second born
Bears his father's name
From humble roots
You produced a tree of pride
Evoking praises to Papa God
Whom you knew from youth
A star born in my homeland

Our second child
Raised in my country of origin
A traveller round the world
Blessing humanity
Through his engineering career
Very far from home
But ever near in my heart
Obeyed God's command
Took a worthy wife and multiplied
A woman of faith and honour
Found favour with God
Blessed with two after his kind
May they grow in wisdom, stature and favour

Obeyed God's command
Honoured his parents
You and your precious wife's days will be long
Your generation will be

Taught of the Lord
Like you both, they will be
Mighty in the land.

May you continue to be
A blessing to your generation
And a light in the world
This is our prayer for you
In the name of our Lord Jesus Christ

Amen.

SILENCE

We sit together
Yet I hear silence
An air of mystery
What thoughts
Cook in your mind?
Yet I hear silence
What images scan your eyes?
Yet I hear silence
What plans hatch in your brain?
Yet I hear silence
We sit together
In our silence
When it is broken
Would our silence
Be peace or war?

LOVE

It is not blue like the sky
It is not red like roses
It is not passion like hearts
It is not riches like gold
It is not green like new grass
It is not silver like money
It is not gratification like sex
It is not warmth like summer
It is not success like spring
It is not merry like autumn
It is not a union like marriage
It is not everything like the world
It is not laughter like comedy
It is not company like friends
It is not hugs like family
Love is sacrifice

CHIDOZIE, OUR THIRD BORN

Arrived seventh year of marriage
When the world greatly panicked
At the milestone dawn of the nineties
A child sent to pamper my every whim:
Papa God, I had asked,
Give me yet another male!
Fair, handsome, godly, and
Like-minded in nature, like my love

A child to grow after Your heart
A lover of nature and animals
A merry soul brimming
With gaiety and humour

A symbol of peace to his siblings
A bringer of fortune
A child of miracles with
Wisdom trailing his years
A generous heart
A man of peace

Papa God, You have granted all this!
He was reluctant to leave You
The extra month in the belly's womb
Necessitated his birth inducement
You marked him out with uncommon marks
You saved him from death's greedy hands
'Olufemi' – You love me, Papa God!

He was wise from birth
Subtle and shrewd but
Gentle and harmless as a dove
Steady in loyalty and sincerity

There is no guile in his heart
Full of love for family
A reliable and devoted friend
Splashes cheers and pleasantry
A humble saint of Christ
To Papa God's glory and our pride

Today, you are a son, man and father
A husband to the woman after your heart
A beautiful helpmate, energetic and devoted

Mighty blessings and unmerited favour will
Surround you both and your children exceedingly

Like the shield from Heaven
May you and your generation
Remain invisible to the enemy and
Fulfil what God has destined for your family

May your wishes be met in Christ
May your desires never be cut short
Your life with your wife and children
Will be full of testimonies and love
You will remain the head and above
You will remain always
A priceless treasure

LIFE ON THE OUTSIDE (inspired by Isaiah 4:6)

Been there,
But I return here
To the booth of my mind
Here I receive shelter
From the heat of the sun's day
And the rain and storms by night
Just like the booths the
Israelites made in the desert
With branches for shade by day
For temperatures over forty degrees high
And the freeze by night
For temperatures below zero degrees

For us in faith
Our Papa God is our booth
Our tabernacle, a place
A shelter, a shade
From the storms of life
When the storms are hitting
From family, work, and life,

I go there to my booth
I talk with Him

Here I receive shelter
I relax with my Papa
I trust Him with all my mind
Whenever I am there
His calmness comes over me
And sorts me out
No matter the heat or freeze
I ask for His help, and He helps me
But when you are outside and
When life happens
Then return inside to the booth of your mind
God is there to give you shelter
And comfort

CHINOMSO, MY SIXTH GRAND

I watch her
A precious gem
From my first blood generation
Visiting for a week
It's half term break

I watch her
Walking on tiptoes
Darting about like a busy bee
I call her name
She denies me her voice

I watch her
She's a little over two
Strong willed, unique, mystifying
An image of her mother
Mischievous eyes avoid mine

I watch her
A gift birthed in May

Carved from mother's belly
Medically received life's first breath
My sixth grand

CHIMA, MY THIRD GRAND

My eyes saw him live
For the first time
He was touching his mouth
Four months old
A little young old man
With his toothless smile

Long before now
My eyes had caressed him in pictures
First half smile,
First full smile
I felt the pride of my son
Having his own son

I felt grateful to God
Not for another grand
Not for my eye's
Or heart's delight
For giving my granddaughter
A brother

My son, his own son
My first grandson
My third grand
He became my son
Grandmother
Becoming mother

THE COUPLE

From breath and dust
Abba made them:
Adam the male,
Eve the female.
They dwelt in Eden

Through their negligence,
Abba's foe deceived them.
For their mistake,
Abba banished them.

United, they found love
They remembered
Abba's commands for survival—
They multiplied
They subdued the Earth
Through the Babel Tower
Eden was sighted…
Abba made Adam Ibo, Eve Yoruba.
Eden was forgotten.

They wanted Eden.
Earth was cursed with
Corruption and Wickedness
They struggled in sweat and pain
Tears and laughter
Earth's sweetness was bitter

Adam blamed Eve.
Eve blamed the Foe.
Eve called to Abba...
Earth became like Eden
The ground was blessed

Earth again turned wicked and corrupt.
Adam spoke to Abba.
Abba heard...
Abba blessed them.
Generations later,
Abba gave them a land
Flowing with Milk and Honey!

THE MYSTERY OF TWO IN ONE

Dark dust daughter of Beatrice from the Midwest
And Augustus from the west
A seed from Nigerian roots
Germinated in London's garden
Reared within Nigeria's west, and gifted to another
By the divine plan of the Master

Fair soil son of Philomina from the east
And son of Patrick from the east
A seed from Nigerian roots reared within Nigeria's
east
Raised and nurtured in Nigeria's garden
And cultivated within Nigeria's west
By the divine will of the Master

Both spiritual seeds grafted by the Master
In the University of Life's Eden
Son of the timber merchant and farmer
Daughter of the lecturer and lawyer
Sprouting fruits of love for another generation
By the divine command of the Master

ECO FRIENDLY

Easy to know if you are:
Are you conscious of
Protecting your environment?
Are you leaving the environment
Better than you found it?

Are you helping to
Make a waste free world?
Are you contributing to plans
To clean oceans?
Are you a part of
Ensuring a stable climate?

Do you use
The likes of Eco stoves?
Are you fighting
Climate pollution?
Are you using
Low carbon materials?
Are you transforming
Pollution to essential produce?

Are you educating yourself
To prepare a stable future?

Have you started what it takes:
To reduce forest fires?
To reduce storms?
To reduce drought?
To reduce landslides?
To reduce flooding?
To reduce unprecedented temperatures?
To reduce animal extinction?
To reduce plant extinction?

Is your voice condemning:
Human trafficking?
Slavery?
Prejudice?
Racism?
Sexism?
Poverty?
Greed?
Corruption?
Selfishness?
Brainwashing?
Knife crime?
Gun crime?

Injustice?
Abuse?
Drugs?
Cults?
Gang Crime?
Bullying?
War?
Discrimination?

We all can do something—
'Charity begins at home.'

Start from your home!

CHIAMAKA, OUR FOURTH BORN

The first female in our family of seven
Patience lies in her wake from Heaven
Waited for three males in the queue ahead
A heart's desire granted
A timely visit since a five year's lap
A strong beautiful princess lands on my lap
Always ahead of milestone expectations:
A walking and talking and schooling babe

At two, competently competing with four-year-olds
She is the Rose of Sharon and the lily of the valley
She is the Ada – first born daughter
She plays with patience to achieve
She enshrouds herself in mystery and charm
Gifted with talent of style and elegance
She is a deep, deep pool – hot and cold
Of secrets, wishes and desires
Excellent with figures and at planning
A socialite at heart with
The daring and boldness of a lioness
Independent like a leopard

Serpentine subtlety with wisdom but
Gentle as a dove
Visible but invisible

She is a blessed daughter
A product of two worlds and nations
A fruit of two personalities
An enchanting smile and talking eyes
In thousands of photographs
And modelled outfits
Loves God at heart and mind

May you continue to increase in grace
May you increase in favour with man and God
May you increase in wisdom and knowledge of God
May he that will complete you
Have the fear and wisdom of God
And be the love of your life
He will be mighty in the land
The fruits of your womb will be
For signs and wonder
You will be a woman of valour
For the kingdom of God
So will this be – Amen!

DEATH

He has passed on
Like a title is passed on
He's gone
Like time is gone
He's left
Like a friend has left
He's dead
Like a battery is dead
He's no more
Like friendship is no more
He's joined his ancestors
Like he's joined a class
He's gone above
Like a balloon has gone above
He has died
Like a plant has died
He has expired
Like a candle has expired
He's breathed his last
Like one has spent his last
He's late

Like a bus was late
He's gone beyond
Like a cloud gone beyond
He's crossed over
Like a tug-of-war crossed over
He's given up the ghost
Like Jesus gave up the ghost
He's kicked the bucket
Like one kicked the beach bucket
He's gone home
Like they've gone for the day
He's gone to be with the Lord
Like he's gone to be with a friend
He's gone to Heaven
Like he's travelled to some city

THE FALL OF KING DAVID (inspired from Isaiah 12:2a)

You had the Garden of Eden
You strolled its vast expanse
Your eyes delighted in creation
Your heart drank its desires
To its contentment
Your physical cup of pleasure
Overflowed in wives and concubines

Your abode surpassed royalty
You tugged on the heart of your Creator
Your talent of plucking the strings
Drew you closer to His heart's string

He clothed you with dripping favour
Adorned your head with royal grace
He followed you to your battles
He gave the kingdom's heart to you

You have come a long way—
The ruddy youth of Bethlehem hills

Feeding and fending your father's flocks
There you battled the bear and wolf
There you perfected the archery of the sling
You learnt meekness from your sheep
You were the lone chorister
Of the hills and plains
Your music of psalms like Abel's offering
Warmed your maker's heart

Your creator forfeited protocol
Bypassed your older siblings
Rejected Saul's heir to the throne
He adorned your head with Israel's crown
You became King of Israel
Like your forefather – Adam
You were asked to enjoy all the blessings
Around you

But you were warned of death
From that single fruit tree
In the Garden of Eden
Enshrouding your creator's ten commandments
You were asked not to eat its fruit

Alas! You ate its fruit
You broke all ten commandments of

Murder, adultery, theft and seven more
Yet beyond your understanding or imagination
He blessed you with Solomon
He honoured your family line
With the world's Redeemer—
God's heir of Salvation

So today,
We all can say
'Behold, God is my salvation,
I will trust
and not be afraid.'

LIFE

It is balanced
on two wheels
the ups and downs

it is held
on two forces
the good and the evil

it is given
on a platter of choices
right and wrong

it is served
into our spirit
for God or Devil

it's seen as complex
in the unknown
and the unknown

it comes in two ways
on the mountains and
in the valleys

it serves our emotion
in two heart chambers
with love and hatred

it comes
in two times
the good and
the bad

CHIASOKA, OUR FIFTH BORN

You complete the family circle of seven,
A child born at the right season—
A birthday gift from God Himself.
A second daughter prayed for
A befitting playmate to the fourth
A younger version of me, people say,
Naturally a gazelle, a doe, a fawn, a dove
But when irked, a spitting volcano

Endowed with true natural beauty of skin and soul
Laughter like the spring brooks
Running on a thousand pebbles
More curious and secretive than a cat
A lover of culture and justice at heart
Loves and reveres God at heart
Deep and mysterious, like a shy virgin
A lover of peace and harmony
Loves the ease and leisure of pleasure
Regally tall and gracefully limbed
She is our *Ulu* – a second daughter
A product of two cultures

Favoured of God with a Midas finger
An adventurer at heart and risk taker
Bears names of both her grandmothers
A lover of babies and pets
A woman who gives respect
Your second half will be perfect for you
Completing you like clasped hands
He will be taught of the Lord
And lift your home to the Lord's heart
Your generation will call you blessed
They will be arrows in your quiver
They will kings and queens and
A light of God in their generation
You and yours will live long and enjoy
God's abundant blessings of favour to the very end

May wisdom guard your heart
And prudence hold tight reins over you
As you excel to the sky's limit
May you walk the path of destiny
Paved perfectly by Papa God
Abraham's blessings will be the portion
Of you and yours—
is our prayer for you.

Amen

ABOUT THE AUTHOR

Olusola Sophia Anyanwu trained as an educationist, teaching English and Literature. She is a reviewer and has reviewed over two hundred books on Amazon and Goodreads. She is an encourager, a bestselling author and poet. She loves reading any book that grabs her attention and interest. In her own words, "I love reading and writing stories that reflect the fascinating and wonderful lives and relationships between the characters." Her writing – in prose and poetry – also conveys current issues in the world.

Being raised in a Christian background has enabled her to write Christian and biblical fiction and poetry. She believes in inspiring people through her writing to understand God's love and awesomeness and to derive encouragement. Her stories and poetry are largely influenced by her faith, which portrays repentance, forgiveness, inclusion, diversity, faith, peace, love for

God, family, and the environment. The Lord Jesus is her inspirer. She is a member of the Association of Christian Writers UK, the Society of Authors UK, National Poetry Library, The Poetry Society UK and TRELLIS Poetry Group UK.

HER WORKS

Olusola Sophia Anyanwu has written twelve books, which include three booklets of poetry. *Poetry Matters* is her fourteenth. As a multi genre author and poet, Sophia has something for everyone: children's stories, romance, historical fiction, adventure, women's fiction, Christian fiction, poetry, biblical fiction, fantasy, and more.

Her poem *Rising* was published in the Association of Christian Writers magazine (winter 2022 edition).

Her poem *God In Love With Me* appeared in *What The Seashell Said To Me: A Collection Of Poems From Sierra Leone* by Bee James (2022).

Her poem *Joseph's Dream* was featured in the Association of Christian Writers blog, *More Than Writers* (January 28, 2023).

In her own words, Olusola Sophia Anyanwu says, "I want my readers to be carried to lofty heights in the realms of passion, love, faith, adventure, and laughter as they read each of my books. So dig in!"

It is her hope that her writing will create a positive influence on readers, enriching their lives, giving encouragement, and blessing every reader.

Olusola Sophia Anyanwu is married and blessed with children and grandchildren. She can be found on Twitter, Facebook, LinkedIn, Amazon, Goodreads, TikTok and Instagram. More information on her and her books can be found on her website:

www.olusolasophiaanyanwuauthor.com

Other poetry books by Olusola Sophia Anyanwu:

Sophia's Covid Poetry
Poetry From The Heart
Chameleon And Other Poems

Printed in Great Britain
by Amazon

27989198R00148